Circe, After Hours

Books by Marilyn Kallet

One for Each Night: Chanukah Tales and Recipes

Sleeping With One Eye Open: Women Writers and the Art of Survival, co-edited with Judith Ortiz Cofer

How to Get Heat Without Fire (poetry)

Worlds in Our Words: Contemporary American Women Writers, co-edited with Patricia Clark

A House of Gathering: Poets on May Sarton's Poetry

Honest Simplicity in William Carlos Williams' "Asphodel, That Greeny Flower"

In the Great Night (poetry)

Last Love Poems of Paul Éluard, translated, with a critical introduction, by Marilyn Kallet

Devils Live So Near (poetry)

The Art of College Teaching: 28 Takes, co-edited with April Morgan

Circe, After Hours

POEMS

Marilyn Kallet

BkMk Press
University of Missouri-Kansas City

BkMk Press
University of Missouri-Kansas City
5101 Rockhill Road
Kansas City, Missouri 64110
(816) 235-2558 (voice); (816) 235-2611 (fax)
bkmk@umkc.edu / www.umkc.edu/bkmk

Financial support of this book has been provided by the Missouri Arts
Council, a state agency.

Cover art: Carole Connely
Cover Photo: Reflections & Images
Book design: Susan L. Schurman
Managing editor: Ben Furnish
Associate editor: Michelle Boisseau
BkMk Press wishes to thank Bill Beeson, Michelle Brownlee,
J. J. Cantrell, and Michael Nelson.

Library of Congress Cataloging-in-Publication Data

Kallet, Marilyn.
        Circe, after hours : poems / Marilyn Kallet
           p. cm.
  Includes bibliographical references.
  ISBN 1-886157-51-0 (pbk.)
     1. Jews--Poetry. 2. Holocaust, Jewish (1939-1945)--Poetry.
     I. Title.

PS3561.A41664 C57 2005
811'.54—dc22   2004028335

This book is set in Klang MT and Adobe Jenson Pro.

For Lou and Heather, always,
and in memory of the Schwarzes of Horb

Acknowledgments

Over the last twenty-five years, the Virginia Center for the Creative Arts has provided a haven for my poetry; the Mary Anderson Center for the Arts has also offered a retreat for writing and reflection. Some of these poems were composed at Squaw Valley Community of Writers, a transformative place for poets. Quotations in "Where Identity Doesn't Rest" are from Brenda Hillman's 1996 craft lecture at Squaw Valley. I am grateful to Dr. John Zomchick for encouragement, to the John C. Hodges Better English Fund as well as to the University of Tennessee College of Arts and Sciences, and to the university Office of Research, for support of this book. The Knoxville Arts Council and the Tennessee Arts Commission provided an individual artist's grant. Dr. Julia Demmin, Elaine Zimmerman, Alice Friman, Barbara Bogue, Libby Falk Jones, Kathryn Stripling Byer, and Deanna Kerns Ludwin provided support and advice. Master craftsman and colleague Arthur Smith offered steady encouragement. Ben Furnish, Robert Stewart, and Michelle Boisseau, editors at BkMk Press, proved to be "real" editors—funny, intelligent, involved. Susan Schurman and Carole Connely have lent their artistic talents to this project; composers Tom Cipullo and David Del Tredici, as well as soprano Melanie Mitrano, have honored my work by setting some of the poems to music.

Poems on family history and the Holocaust were supported by grants from the Graduate School of the University of Tennessee. At the United States Holocaust Memorial Museum, Kelly Skovbjerg and Peter Lande helped me to trace family records. Rabbis Howard Simon and Tom Gutherz translated the Hebrew of Pinkas Hakellot pertaining to Horb. Rabbi Beth Schwartz offered moral support. Joan Acocella wisely pointed me to *Austerlitz*, by W. G. Sebald, which inspired me and lent courage for the research at Theresienstadt. I am indebted to University of Tennessee Professor Gilya Schmidt for her research on rural Jewish life in Rexingen; to Professor Peter Hoeyng, for his assistance in planning my trip to Germany. Ulrich Struve of the University of Freiburg facilitated my research in Germany. Adolf Sayer in Rexingen, Manfred Stek in Horb, Bernhard Wochner and Mayor Rolf Kiefer in Mühringen, all provided information about Jewish life in Swabia. The Sisters at Marienhospital in Stuttgart were gracious and helpful; their predecessors were my great-aunt's angels in 1945. My family is very grateful.

Some of these poems have been previously published.
Grateful acknowledgement is made to the editors.

"Twilight Sleep," *Appalachian Life*
"Bodily Harm," "Tomato Frog," *Asheville Poetry Review*
"Bumper Boats," *Sport Literate*
"It Can't Happen," *Connecticut Review*
"Global," *Ironhorse Quarterly Review*
"Grits," *The Ledge*
"Where Identity Doesn't Rest," "To My Poem of Hope," "Out of
          Silence," *New Letters*
"Trout" ("German Phone Sex"), "Circe, Did You?" "Monsieur Moreau,"
          "Horb," *New Millenium Writings*
"Jealous," *Now & Then*
"The Ladies," *Potomac Review*
"Finally," "No Makeup," "Missing Heather," "Turning Your Death
          into Ralph Lauren," "Hedwig's Story" (first version),
          "Horb" (first version), *Prairie Schooner*
"No Sale," *Tar River Poetry*
"On the Night Train," *Traffic Report*
"Warning," *Whole Terrain*

"Bumper Boats" appeared also in *Breathing the Same Air: An East
Tennessee Anthology* (Celtic Cat).

"Hedwig's Story" and "Survivor" appeared also in *Migrants &
Stowaways: An Anthology of Journeys* (Knoxville Writers Guild).

"Heartland, Revisited" appeared also in *Knoxville Bound* (MetroPulse).

Contents

III. Breathing Daughters

The sea is cold without love.

—Paul Éluard

I
Trout

Warning

No Swimming Except
with a Franciscan Friar
—sign posted at
Mount Saint Francis Lake

No plunging your
body into the cool lake
no letting the water lilies

caress your breasts
no letting the trout
nibble your toes

no fanning out
your hair
no floating on your back

wind whispering
over fevered skin
except with a Franciscan.

Alice warned me
"No Swimming Except
with a Franciscan" was taken

by another poet.
No writing about
no swimming

except with a
Franciscan friar.
No writing no swimming with

Robert Hass
Robert Pinsky

Robert Frost

the Lakers
or Gwendolyn Brooks.
No reading this poem

about no swimming
without a Brother.
It might lure you in.

When I asked Brother Tim
if he'd go swimming
he was agreeable.

"Since I lost my swimming buddy
Mimi, I haven't been in."
How did he lose his

swimming buddy Mimi?
No drowning without
a Franciscan friar—

better yet, not
without a priest.
No swimming

with Holy Rollers
Mennonites
or Chasids.

(Brothers: no pretending
to walk on water
by striding

across the old
barely submerged
dam.)

When I asked
Brother Tim
how I could be sure

he was really
a Franciscan
and could he show me

some ID
he assured me he'd taken
his vows in 1983.

No babies
in baskets
by the bullrushes

without a friar
no chicken picnics
in the canoe.

Insurance can be
costly. Remember
what happened

to Mimi.

Trout

Beau is babbling about German phone sex,
a pro on the cover of some slick highbrow mag
mouthing "Give it to me!"
in her gutteral tongue.

My phone sex in German
would be short.
I recall only the ditty
about the irritable trout:

Ziemlich schlecht,
sagt der Hecht,
in der Tiefe
Liebesbriefe.

Bad news,
said the sea trout,
in his love letter
from the deep.

Bad news is not what customers
pay to hear.
Bad news, all I remember from that summer
with the Nazi at Columbia,
German 101, drinking songs at 8 A.M.,
hoisting *du, du* . . . alone
in the language lab.

Beau and I struggle
with two different languages.
He speaks twenty-year-old WASP on his way
to the regatta,
the rap of a beautiful man
on his way to any woman he damn well chooses.
I talk fifty-year-old wife and mother,

Jewish teacher, for whom German jokes don't
come easy.

Jews don't sail,
I want to tell him.
We put an ocean between us and the Cossacks.
Kept our feet on city sidewalks after that.
But for Beau I might put on a life jacket.
I might take summer lessons like an
underprivileged trout.

I'd let him teach me waves,
call him Captain,
O, Captain.

"No! You wouldn't seriously
consider it?"
my old friend Bill exclaimed.
"That would be grotesque."

At forty-five, Bill himself
had a fling with Jan
the teenaged painter
who gave phone sex to pay her rent.
Jan was something of a sailor.
She could only come underwater.
For Bill, that was a summer
of Great Lakes.

Great art is grotesque, no?
Think of Picasso.
Think of anything but a young man
with his looks and his poetry
his music and his crooning
his painting and his and his
mouth-watering
trout.

No Makeup

"Makeup can only do so much,"
Marco at Bendel's said
when I went for my wedding consultation.
He would try.
To bulk up the fairy tale aura
 he glued my Turquoise and Candlelight lids
with spidery lashes.
Presto! Piled on a braided hairpiece,
a kind of hairy *challah*.

When I walked down the aisle
that first time, 1969,
the year of Zeffirelli's
Romeo and Juliet,
I was a vision of loneliness.
My father, who offered
under his breath, "You don't have to
marry him," gave me away.
I didn't get stoned until the reception
where drunk Uncle Sammy
pulled down his pants.
(It's on the video.)

But what happened at the motel
was no joke. I pulled off
the hair and eyes.
Marriage!
With a man whose body
made me cringe
as if I was the ingenue
facing Fatty Arbuckle.
I couldn't hide.
Prayed for him

to fall asleep early.

Why did I marry him?
At twenty, who knew about being born?
Mother insisted I was lucky
to find someone who loved me.
"A miracle," she crooned,
"a Jewish doctor."

"I'd rather die than marry him,"
I said.
"Then die," she said.
Three years and I was ready to jump
from our Stuy Town window.

I was rescued by a cowboy
and a Jungian.
In one dream,
my mother, sister and I
wore wedding dresses in a rowboat
at sea. "There's Moby Dick!" I yelled.
"Row back to shore
for the wedding!" Mother ordered.
"You go," I said.
"I have to stay here and fight."

I left him.
The next years
made sexual history.
I'm no shaman, but I've lived and died
many times, and here I am singing.

This morning, a raccoon
looked in the mirror
after a night of writing.

"Makeup can only do
so much," I thought.
"I'll have to rely on poetry,
won't I?"
And how, at fifty, I love
nakedness
in my face and lines,
and in your hands, dear reader.

Monsieur Moreau

Monsieur Moreau must be dead by now.
He was the *père de famille*
of the household where I boarded,
in 1967, Avenue du Parc Montsouris.

One evening, during the family supper,
Monsieur reminisced about the day
the Paris police arrived at the factory
where he worked, and "took away the Jews."

"*Les juifs.*" He giggled. I
swallowed, the leek soup, an onion.
In her black dress,
Madame looked like a crow.

They were hard workers,
la bourgeoisie,
solid, Monsieur and Madame.
Both of them must be dead by now.

Paris is beautiful, no question.
Et oui, vive la Résistance!
Paris hated the Nazis, *les boches.*
At the auto plant, no one hid Jews.

Beneath his little clownlike mustache,
Monsieur giggled.
No question.
Perhaps he died in his bed, quietly,

on the *belle* Avenue du Parc Montsouris.

The Hedgehog

Sheila says, "The little hedgehog lives
in the shade of the mulberry tree."
I'm back at Madame's table, 1967.
She's serving unchewable grey meat.

In my best student French
I offer, "*C'est délicieux, Madame,
Mais, qu'est-ce que c'est?*"
("Great stuff—what is it?")

"*C'est du hérisson.*"
The word shuddered.
After supper, I rushed
to my Larousse—

Hedgehog! Next day
I queried my French friends,
"Is it a delicacy?"
"*Mais <u>non</u>!*"

Madame, by now you cook no more.
But the hedgehog lives on.
Your crimes were small, mostly
committed at table.

I'm told you served
petit âne for Christmas, a sweet
little ass from Montmartre. Alas,
I left Paris before the festivities.

Did Monsieur help you carve?
"*Tais-toi, tu m'embêtes!*"
you'd yell at him, stunned beast,

each night after soup.

Might I mention dessert, the night
you handed us boarders a bowl of lemons
urging, *"Prenez! Prenez!"*
You insisted that we each eat one.

I paid you back, didn't I,
murdering your language
each time I opened my hungry
Yankee mouth.

Great Poet

I was a great poet, composed,
understated, subdued.
Never let personality leak
into a syllable.
I wrote psalms with my silences.
Remember that jar in Tennessee?
Its curves, an indulgence.
I was a shard washed translucent
by the ocean. Glinting,
I whispered prophecies.

One day, by accident, on I-75 South,
I switched to Lucinda Williams
on the radio. My psyche spilled over
like a fleshy spare tire. I remembered
that my father sculpted his fingernails.
My mother cursed like a lumberjack.
My sister was demonically possessed
by her own curriculum vita.
I let go. Suddenly
Walt Whitman made sense—I rolled
along with him ticking off the miles.
Woody Guthrie hummed, sweeter than angels.
And Bob Dylan? He was God.

When Hazel Dickens came on
wailing, "My soul, my soul,"
the hair on my arms stood up.
Then I realized I wasn't a pearl.
I had hair.
I must be animal.
I embodied a soul.
Still, I found myself unable to say
"postmenopausal."

Beau

Je suis belle, ô mortels! comme un rêve de pierre...
—*Baudelaire*

Jewish mothers do not name their sons Beau.
We call them Milty or Sammy or Mel
so that when one comes along
whose name exclaims his beauty
and that beauty, forbidden to my tongue

Summons a landscape of handsome
well-crafted men
performing heroic acts
sailing tall ships into Ilion
or regattas out of Charleston—

When the name of Beauty comes along
and it is very young
one must be careful
to sing it
sparingly.

Inside his poems
dreams a man more beautiful than his name
whose vulnerability is more thrilling
than his machismo, whose words
rescue me from the ordinary—

Beau, teach me to live in language again
to plant the flag on the unforgiving line
that time has drawn between us
to never speak of it,
never step over.

No Sale

How would a Jewish girl
sell her soul to the Devil?
Reformed don't believe
in Beezlebubba.

Now Robert Johnson, he
had no such trouble.
You know the tale, how the bluesman
sold his soul at the crossroads

for a lifetime of hot-lick guitar.
Shot by a jealous husband
at the roadhouse, he died on his knees
they say, drunk, barking like a dog.

Odd, for a nice Jewish girl
to fall on her knees.
Years though, that's how
it was. Me shot down,

baying at the moon
for a lick of you.

Heartland, Revisited

Why do we hope for more than we can bear?
Me, wanting to meet Dante in a dream!
He could be a duck for all I'd understand.
Nights you're trading secrets
with Rimbaud. In poetry you want me,
not slow like Beatrice, hot
like fast food.
I'm old enough to be your Meemaw.
You chase me like a puppy yapping after a car.
If I turned around? Some crush
you'd have then. Honey, I'm taking
hormone replacement therapy.
You're pure testosterone.
I can't take you.

You come to my office hungover, red-eyed,
too young, still my suitor.
You're craving
songs. I'm the dealer.
Sweetheart, you're the source
of your own uncut lines.
Pure poetry? Runs
from the underside
of your life, raw—fistfight
with your stepfather, sneaking out
of his house in a stolen car,
into the arms of your jailbait lover.
At fifty-five, all I can give is
advice. You hug my words as if I'm her.

I'm hypnotized by your lips,
place where your voice emerges.
I ditched the CD, fled

your crooning.
You're not my old friend Orpheus,
the one I lost to the white lady,
you're not the other,
who lured me halfway through
hell before bolting, leaving me
to sing my own way out.
Hell was an unfinished basement,
a Sweet Sixteen party that didn't take off.
We gnawed on my mother's sweated-over fried chicken
and watched a dinky magician. You're not him.

Orpheus grew up in Jackson, moved east to UT.
Sported a black helmet, parked his Harley
near Europa and the Bull. He was Redford
in *The Natural*—women couldn't pop
their eyes back in. We fell for his silky
yellow hair, his swiveling bag
of tricks. He hummed Elvis
and we held our breath.
Girls worshipped the back
of his golden head. Orpheus
took off for Arizona and his M.F.A.
Dug up a rock band and junk instead.
His face crumpled like Jim Morrison's
at the end. Still, no one left the room.

Orpheus was a dark-haired Virginian
with no excuses. Rich like Blue Ridge soil.
Smooth as prime tobacco. Swift and hard
like highway machinery chomping on mountains.
So beautiful even a flowering pear
bent a little with envy.
Orpheus the homewrecker, swollen magnolia,
music of excess and falling silk.
Even his ghost holds sway over us.

I still search for him at the Fresh Market,
near tomatoes where I'd caught a glimpse.
Perfectly absent as if dead,
he's out there,
his old Br'er Fox Boomsday Sleight-of-Hand self.

What satisfaction can'st thou have if
you're a kid and I'm a married woman?
Write. Pick your words like sweet corn
from a well-fertilized garden.
These are your natural resources: wit,
a loving spirit, a good ear.
And those lips.
Aren't they the heartland?
I admire from afar, touch nothing.
Dear Orpheus, listen:
Euridice sings too. She knows more
about dark sweet earth,
how to plant deep and sure—
more than the strumming boys do.

Circe, Did You?

Circe, like those siren sisters you warned of,
did you croon men to your shore?
Did you surround-sound sailors with silky hair
and nipples? *Oooh*, when you stroked them
with syllables, did it matter to your tongue
who they were? Or were you waiting for one,
Odysseus, with his many-skilled fingers?
In the ruby-tipped dawn did you hold out
for the master mariner, craving mutual song?
Had you dreamed his lure of black hair,
called out his snake-charmer's name, long after
you had previewed that shaggy-dog ending?

Sometimes names trick us into dreams
of having. *Odysseus*,
an undercurrent, a squall.
Hurricane Odysseus.
Circe, blown away.

Tomato Frog

You're so vain,
You probably think this song is
about you.
　　　　　　　—Carly Simon

He must have been a god, the one
who cross-bred a tomato with a frog.
Long ago, tomatoes had a hard time
getting around. If they wanted to party,
they could never rock, only roll.
Smashed, they squished.

Once amphibious, they called the shots.
All that gorgeous *rouge*
on the move! Green frogs bulged with envy.
Nothing as alluring on blue sand
as a red jumper posed *au naturel*.

Famous painters would steamer
to Madagascar to catch a glimpse
of one. Gauguin himself revered
bold skin, aimed to compose them
amid Goddess's nipples.
No still life there.

In this portrait, froggy's wide-eyed,
goofy, more humble than you might allow.
His ancestors were sliced for sandwiches
(we musn't speak of that).
Now he evades the barbaric nets
of chefs. "Out of the produce bin,
into the frying pan? *Non! Jamais!*"
Red has become royalty-waiting-to-happen.
Red-lipped women have leaned
to kiss him. . .

"I have my own career now.
I'm tired of being used
by girls on their way up."
Older women try harder
to capture one.
Not that they want a prince,
no way, they're thinking show biz,
value—a talking frog.

Our red buddy (call him
Big Boy for old time's sake)
is adjusting to his new body.
"Like an artiste, I leap,
I plunge. I'm
the first generation
to land on my feet!"

 When he has nightmares of toasters
and bacon he wakes up shrieking
his wife *croaa-bits*
over his rippled skin
until he sheds smoothness,
the vine,
the old days
dangling in Farmer Jones's patch
like a Christmas ornament.
"Like one engorged testicle,"
he shudders.

Darling, you too were blatant,
over-kissed, elusive.
You were the local Big Boy,
everyone's delicious pet.
How we wanted to bite
into you! Until you pissed
in our hands. Until you cowered

under rocks. We noticed
our grasping fingers were covered
with telltale warts.

Cat Mummy

And, even if wars didn't keep coming like glaciers,
there would still be plain old death...
　　　　　　　　—Kurt Vonnegut

1

Nothing plain about your death, old soul.
Your ears bound, your nose and gut
crammed with gauze.
You were royal. Not even Ramses Junior
threw rocks at you. You possessed
your own slave, like my cat Jacques.
So what went wrong? Ramses' hawk
swooped down on your juicy eyes. No?
Maybe you sat too long, fattened by mouse liver,
goat cream. You grew slow, couldn't leap
onto Ramses' lap. They wound you back
like an anti-clock.
As if bandages could stop you from running off.

2

Jews don't do mummies. Who has time?
No graven images, no fetishizing.
Not even a tattoo. Though sometimes,
when one of us falls in love, we forget,
fall out of line, on our knees. Bound
by our own desires, our hands
are tied, and it's a good thing, otherwise
we'd make a god of our beloved,
retrace creation on his skin,
with our lips, our tongue.
Good thing memory's not taboo,
isn't it, dark one?

3

"I've been married twice and both wives
wanted money," Kurt Vonnegut complained,
at the Student Center dinner.
"I only want to be loved for myself,
but that's impossible now."

He's chewing cheesecake, searching
for a Hemingway title.
Wiping cream from his mustache,
he finds it: *Farewell to Arms.*

"Now *that* was a great love affair!"
he said. "Thank God she died!"

Out of Silence, for Sister Wendy

Sister Wendy says that Perugino's Magdalene
gleams shallow, not ready for the light.
To me she radiates heat like a ripe peach,
all fragrant lushness—I suspect
her inner life's a red herring.
But I'm a Reformed Jew, and Sister
knows her silences, more surely
than Magdalene, mere teenager.
I only balk when those young New Lifers
claim Christendom's a higher bargain
than our Old-Time Religion. I want
to dangle little *dybbuks* at them
from my rearview mirror.
And wasn't Perugino a chocolate-maker?

No peace last night, Sister,
though I climbed in bed with your book,
aware of the shallow nature
of my reflections, my silence thin
as the top sheet on lasagne. From
downstairs strains of Christmas
carols blasted my ears.
The roar of the hallway heater
took over and I descended into dreams
of poet Z, starring arty home
improvements, Tweedledee the coke dealer
cradling an Uzi, my breathstealing
dash for the closet—reprieve!
I could slide the bolt shut inside.

Clever poet had prepared
for this, his carpentry a shelter.
He'd crafted a thick plank

of dark oak between dream-self
and danger. Sister Wendy says the gate
between us and divine silence
must be unlocked. We can only
admire the beauty of alertness
for so long. We should stay poised
for our penultimate push toward bliss.
Ready with spiritual rockets,
we'll be armed against our terror.
Then what engine will thrust the dreamer
out on her celestial ear?

Z's dream house also harbored
Caligari's cabinet, a wobbly
ellipsoidal toilet, its sink stopped
with rusty water. Either I've neglected
the unconscious in my New York rush
toward God, or dreaming dubious waters
of grace, in the night I had to pee.
The plumbing in that old house
hadn't wed the carpentry. The body
chastens us, don't you find,
when we try to walk a spiritual line
without offering libation, without
scaring preschool Isaac witless, poor ram.

"New York rush toward God" catapults
memory to September eleventh.
Small silence has been invoked
to help us grieve.
A moment here, there. Our President
does the best he can, launching one
sentence. Then another. Months,
and young Deena who cried, "I'll never trust
the sky again!" wails trying to find sleep.
What can we cull from still life

to soothe the children
stunned by violence? Help us, Sister,
to find words as illuminated
as your treasured *White Lilac* by Manet.

We pattern-making animals love endings,
yet there's no cut and dried.
Good St. Catherine praises eternity
through her rapturous gaze by Raphael.
If we could ride her eyebeams heavenward
with our Italian boots on, we'd be happy.
You claim true silence demands more of us.
We must wait actively, like Coltrane,
with *Love Supreme*. Then even the buzz of the heater
will permit us to unbind particulars
and live in sound's equivalent to light.
A pity, me so attached to my things—
my gloves, my red pocketbook, ghost
sonnets—these humble love songs to you.

The Blessing of Hair

Brother William is the youngest friar
in the province, and if you ask him
where he's from, he'll claim, "Heaven!"
I believe him, admire the gleam
of his olive skin, his thick, shiny hair.
To others, he'll admit "San Salvador."

When Barb sighed, "Oh, your hair is beautiful!"
he blurted, "Then you must touch it!"
"Oh," she swooned, "His hair is holy!"
I almost believe it, those black curls
luminous. Though he's God's,
he loosened his hair down his back for Barb.

What a blessing, his mane unfurling
across his shoulders. "It's a
wonder!" he declares. It's a wonder
the other friars don't lock him away,
this brother from heaven, with his purple
lips, this young one who loves prayer.

He used to write poetry, he confessed,
"In Spanish. Romantic and sexy.
But that was B.C.!"
(Wish I'd known him then.)
I volunteered to translate his verses.
"No, no! The friars might not understand."

His English is near-perfect.
He offered to bring us dessert,
and when I asked for a pear
he brought me a Bud Light.
Brother William, when you brush out

your hair, be careful

what you imagine, keep watch
over your dreams. Do not savor
the women poets seated near you
in the friary cafeteria. Keep
that B.C. boy under wraps.
Young lion, let your hair gleam

for God only, may it grow
for a blessing,
let it net only souls,
this silky obsidian
legacy of your Mayan mother,
your miraculous unsacrificed hair.

It Can't Happen

Not now not ever
not at your house, your living room,
your couch, not in the late afternoon
not while my husband's waiting
my daughter's on hold
not at my house not in the hot tub
not with wine coke or dope
not with Mexican, Colombian, hydrotropic, not
now.

Not in my office
on my desk
not in the meadow under stars
not with whiskey or Ecstasy
not in this lifetime not now.

Not unless
you fall down on your knees
not unless you cry, bleed, beg
not unless our lips brush
not unless your caress blots out memory
not unless you're bigger than your myth
not unless you've grown braver
not unless your hair's still curly
not unless you write a poem for me
and slam it hard enough to kill reverie
not unless you call me
write to me
not now not ever not unless.

II
Bumper Boats

Twilight Sleep

(after reading Heaney's Electric Light*)*

When Seamus Heaney's *deeply cargoed* sailor
spread his wet clothes in the sun
we gasped with delight. When Mommy
hung heavy sheets on our backyard lines
in Oceanside, only the wind clapped.

Unlike Anglo-Saxon mommies, mine
never swore my friends were *heathen brutes.*
Nebbocks! she deemed the men I dated. Poets!
She was right to be scared. Mostly they were
meshugganah. Steve, the Jewish doctor,
she liked. Three years out of my life.

Unlike baby Seamus, at my birth
no hearty Doctor Kerlin came round.
That nice Doctor Monsky from Montgomery
delivered. Ma never glimpsed his busy hands.
Those days hospitals dispensed with memory.
Say what you will about the womb's
natural opium, in '46 the docs shot raving
moms with dope. Forgetting is almost
as important as remembering, even now,
women and salt-washed sailors don't doubt.

Bumper Boats

1

Today we spend our mortality
waiting in line for bumper boats.
Not everything can be a metaphor.
Not in this racket. *Zing!*
Zowee! Zeus and Hera zap
metallic innards of video machines
and mine while they're at it. Kids scream.

Good times with Mom! Fast memories!
I break the speed limit spending
on my ten-year-old and her friend.
"Do we have to go home now, Mommy?
No more tokens?
This stinks!"

"Look at all those life-jackets
for three feet of water!
This is stupid!"

A foghorn belches 900 miles inland.

2

Sundays my father would treat my sister
and me to kiddie rides at Nunley's.
I'd rush to the robot fortune-teller.
She was no Blavatsky but I loved her.
For a penny her ruby-tipped fingers
turned the cards—I lost myself
in her glass eyes and china lips,
dropping my future when it finally shot out.
And the carousel, the rings that I almost

killed myself trying to grab. Every kid knows
there *is* one free ride if you're willing
to break your neck for it.

"You'll remember me after I'm dead,"
my father would intone, at Nunley's.
And I do, remember him driving us home
after rides and hot dogs,
days when I'm schlepping in circles,
waiting in line with Heather and Glynis
til it's their turn to get soaked
in bumper boats
up to their prepubescent gills.

Jealous

Mount Saint Francis Lake

I'm jealous of those parents.
Their goslings gliding in a line
between stately Mom and Dad
don't suddenly turn and announce
"I want to go to Interlochen!"

Goslings don't yearn to play
marimba. They don't fly
to snowy Michigan and leave
bereft parents in Knoxville.

It won't cost the farm
to send them to gliding
and honking school.
Alone, their mother and father
won't suddenly turn
to one another and think,
"What now?"

After their kids go
these two will sail
the cool water,
shit on the dock,
eat bugs.
The lake buoying them
will remind them
of their own mother,
her unflappable calm, her
noisy temper flaring
when foxes crept
or humans stomped down to the edge.

Their wings will recall ancestral
flight patterns.
There will be no nostalgia,
no twinges in the feathers,
no grabbing ankles and pulling down.

Bodily Harm

When Libby's twenty-pound boa
struck at the rat, I dropped my tea
on her snowy carpet.

Long as a squirrel, the white rat
had been frozen.
Libby's husband reheated it
in the microwave (where I had been
thinking of warming my tea.)

Boa embraced her rat dreamily.
If you didn't know
she was choking what she
thought was a live one,
you would have guessed she adored him.

I warmed to them.
She reminded me of Tom
from Utica, that all-too-tight
embrace, how I'd have to explain
when he caught me talking to a man.
To be fair, we took turns strangling,
being rats.

So that when he came after me,
when the New York State police
rang me with "We don't want to
alarm you, but . . ."
I was scared, but not stunned.

Luckily he stopped himself
en route with a butcher knife.
Married now, him to a

nurse from Brooklyn, me
to a regular Joe
who doesn't lunge at pets
we've both got all the hugging
we can swallow.

Pedo Pantoum

"All the pedophiles are living at the gun shop,"
Sheryl, the cook, smirked at the friary lunch.
This tidbit of gossip was her offering.
Giftshop volunteers giggled at our table.

Sheryl, the cook, offered up hot news
about the old gunshop at the corner.
Volunteers and gifted writers giggled.
We adore Brother Jay, and were distressed.

He's living in the gunshop at the corner.
A tiny gun and bait shop—how do all the pedophiles
fit in? We love Brother Jay, and don't believe
rumors. Those who dwell in the Gun and Bait:

tidbits. Gossip is Sheryl's gift.
All the pedophiles are living in her breath.

On the Night Train, Out of Montgomery

I wet the sheets
    in the Pullman car
        woke up   wailing
            "sauerkraut!"

"Want sauerkraut!" too few words
    to tell Grandma
        I meant the song
            Mommy rocked me with—

"Where was Moses
    when the light went out?
        Down in the cellar
            eating sauerkraut."

Why? No one told me why
    we were fleeing.
        "New York,"
            they said.

"We can't take Buffy.
    An apartment   might not want us
        with a dog."
            We pulled away—

Buffy watched us from the lawn
    I screamed   with the train
        Grandma finally sang to me
            Where was Mommy

when the lights went out?
    Few words and none for
        terror
            "bye bye"—

and the world ends?
    Grandma sang   and I slept.
      Maybe it's true
        we must go back

before loss of Mother
    to the sound the wind made
      through the tunnel
        before the sleepingcar entered

to the silence
    Coltrane might have tasted
      before he blew *A Love Supreme.*
      Before our sorrow

maybe the earth was waiting
    for wet creatures
      like me and Buffy
        to touch its back—

waiting for song   in the night train
    calmer now   I have words
      to soothe my shattered heart
      and exiled body.

Fishing With Bloodworms

How my father, a Brooklyn boy,
came to fishing I don't know;
or how my mother, Southern belle
with stiff hair, found her taste
for it, unless she picked up
bait and pole to lure him.

In a snapshot of me at three,
puffed out in a white dress,
a tiny fish dangles from my line.
My father hooked the sunfish
while my back was turned.
Mommy flirts in the background.

After our exile to Long Island,
my little sister and I
were packed into the car
for Candlewood Lake.
Daddy started yelling
before he turned the engine on.

Those days he sold used cars.
He needed a sturdy roof,
so nothing would fall on him.
But one day he snagged the loaner,
"the boat," a red Chevy convertible.
We kids leaned back and cruised heaven.

At the lake Mommy baited all our hooks.
We felt her piercing of wiggling
fat flesh was disgusting,
though we were awed by her.
We'd fish for hours,

thrilled by the bob-and-pull.

Once, riding home with the top down,
my sister and I curled up in the back,
huge crabs we'd landed by mistake
scurried out of a basket on the floor,
us screaming, my father screeching
to the roadside.

Even now crawling things
come after me in my dreams.
My father long gone, my mother
one year buried. But I see them
with their bamboo poles and
freshly baited hooks.

In the morning mist
a young couple drifts off in a rowboat.
"Any luck?" I call out.
They lean into their lines,
the way willows bow
over the glittering lake.

Scorpions

Like Rockettes they centered themselves
in my childhood living room
on our blue Persian rug.

"Who are you?" I asked the biggest one.
"I'm darkness hardened,
your fear unspoken,
what you thought you had left behind.
You can run..."

If death is the mother of beauty,
why does it smash us
just as we start crawling?

Mother, after we buried you,
Elaine and I tried to replant
your red begonias at the grave.
Fire ants bit my fingers.
It was hard to breathe.
A benadryl saved me—pills
didn't fix you, did they?

Still, I miss that blue rug of memory.
Oh, to have you back
in your soft blue robe!

Doesn't the mommy scorpion
love her little ones?
The ones too young for words
who dread the living room,
dread breaking the "lady lamp"
you carried from Alabama to New York,
your "one beautiful thing."

Scared of your crying.
Scared of my being five years old
and never being forgiven.

Not so little now, creatures
the size of rock lobsters.
Huddled like all-stars.

If you are angels, come dancing in
through some crack in the dream-window

fractured by my mother's death,
why shouldn't I fear you?
Archaic ghosts randomly spirited
from the silted floor,
why should I listen?

On Vincent Street, we had no money
and the Oriental rug wore bare.
My mother sat me down with an
India-ink pen. For hours I darkened
the teeming white threads.
Me against time, against shabbiness,
me the foe of Mother's misery
at losing Southern gentility.

Ancient crawling ones,
scurrying over the inky surfaces
of childhood,
you can't hear me
on the flip side of time.

Angels of otherness, if you find
my mother, tell her I'm sorry
in your succulent no-words,
our nightly collaborative tongue.

The Hit

In Brooklyn there must have been no lawn
and little bread, so when we made it

to Long Island, Daddy fed the birds.
"No, no, no!" he'd cry, if I threw crusts.

"You have to tear the pieces into crumbs."
He pretended not to know the Mob.

When the don invited him to Atlantic City
with the "Family," Daddy answered,

"I'll have to see if my wife has plans."
Good for a laugh. Clean,

Dad lent cover.
Before they threatened him.

"Pull your vending machines out of that bar,
or we'll kill your wife and children!"

their goon growled on the phone.
"No!" Daddy said. So they sent a guy

disguised as the gas man
to grab me and my sister.

Wiretaps caught the hit
before they whacked us.

Daddy made a cleancut witness.
A shame he never got the chance to vote.

Did I mention that he was a felon?
He was framed.

Just a businessman.
Good-looking hustler, no crook.

In '66, Senator Javits
secured a pardon for my Dad.

Bobby Kennedy would have signed it, too,
but someone sent a guy after him.

Daddy died anyway from smoking Lucky Strikes.
Dark-haired, like me,

he was the one who named me "Marilyn."
We hardly ever saw him.

After late-night stops in Brooklyn
he'd leave chocolate jelly rings

in our "Good Fairy Bowl."
Mornings when I feed the birds

I'm his daughter again, scattering crumbs
like secrets, or ashes.

Where
identity doesn't rest

memory, you adorable
squid you, squirting poetry—

pen-skid down the back
alley, whatever

the destination the same,

where the unknown would have been
       our childhood backyards   we use
          flotation   as
                                  anchors

What if memory were only the
                      arms of now?
If memory is only
the study of memory, its suckers   I have to
                                wonder
                                how many

signing the water
things can

                                go wrong

If I have to give up memory
forfeit the three-year old
torn out of Montgomery
  without her dog Buffy
  I swear to you that loss
  that cruelty is oak-solid in me

where will I be?

"I'm as thirsty as
          a wormy old dawg,"
                    I said,
              fell back on my old
                          home
tongue, cozy
the one I was born in,
not this cold New York slap
but the warm mouth of the
Mammy who raised me   my father fired her
(she stopped him from walloping me)
the D.A. hounded my father out of Alabama

four years old in New York kindergarten
I raised my hand for water
"thirsty as a wormy. . ."
their laughter iced me
by spring my drawl had melted
not memory, not memory

                              "the
                               fragment
                               has more to

                               do with
                               nature
                               than not"

bicoastal rush
oak to eucalyptus
aye-ayeing green coins

clichés don't
tremble

and I hold onto that?

fragrant cells
wavering

save me from hating

honestly, there is
identity in
me, like an oak
tree, no, really,

really,
a little *click*-child

"it's the terror and the way
you are falling out."

Turning Your Death into Ralph Lauren

In hell I'll be wearing Ralph Lauren
and you Mother will be yelling
how I have too many clothes.
You'll salt away money.
The Great Depression will
still be on. You'll have to wait
until you're sixty for college.
I'll never delay anything.

Today I bought a luscious
chocolate-covered—I mean
chocolate-colored leather jacket.
"The unconscious is expensive,"
my therapist says.

The truth is (I'm ashamed),
after my mother died
I bagged four leather jackets
on top of a camel sweater,
Ralph Lauren.
One beige skin?
I couldn't get warm.

The brown hide over which
Margo swooned, "It was made for you!
Like a newborn's skin!"
too tender.

Only black leather can restore
the thirteen-year-old self
who yearned to belong to a gang.
(Jewish girls were throwaways

to the Lords and Dukes.)
At fifty-one, I want to be them.
Oh Manny and John!
Blonde angels with switchblades
and roaring bikes.
Like Abe I always had to walk.
I want good boots and a knife in my hand.

Want the jacket that spits on death,
the skin that reads *Connected*.
I want to be zipped into Eros.
To be the one who hotrods
        Sunrise Highway,
not the sitting chick back home.

Don't take away these layers.
Doctors took my mother.
My sister stole her from me
when I was three.
This gutting is worse.
Really, this is worse.

My therapist asks,
"How many dead animals do you
have hanging in your closet now?"

Finally

Finally (one year down) I dreamed my mother
was dead, no, that she was dying.
"My heart has closed," she explained.
This time I was with her,
in the crowded atrium of a school.
This time I helped her to lie down,
ran to find a pillow, but by the time
I came back she was gone,
just a blanket on the floor.

So I chatted with schoolgirls
about pocketbooks—their large, sumptuous
leather bags, their fabulous matching luggage.
"If you can't afford what I have
then you're not a good role model,"
one attractive young woman said.

Maybe it wasn't the medication
that killed her,
or the smug inattentive specialist.
Her heart had been closed to me
for a long time, but she was alive,
wasn't she, she loved my sister,
and my daughter, and I could watch her loving.

I had just been with her for Mother's Day,
driven the long hours to Montgomery.
I was a good daughter, wasn't I?
She was woozy and scared.
The young temp doctor had changed her
heart pills and suddenly she could
feel the beat jumping wildly

and no one would listen.

"What would happen if you didn't go home
right away?" Mother pleaded.
"I have to turn in my grades," I said.
"Oh," she sighed.

Next day the call found me at home.
How they found her on the bathroom floor.
No Southern Lady would have smiled on this.

No daughters.
No blanket and no pillow.

And the luggage? I went on a leather-
buying binge after the ashes.
Credit kept me covered.
Department stores gave me hope.
I could be anyone.
Wasn't I an American?
With the tote bags and satchels
couldn't I carry myself? Why
did I need a mother?

Well stuff my mouth,
as they used to say down home.
Why shouldn't I stuff my closet
with sleek hides instead of howling?

III
Breathing Daughters

Global

Mother would have loved global warming.
A good Alabama girl, she resented
cold Long Island mornings
and my Brooklyn-born father,
who had dragged her North, toward snow.

She'd phone me long distance at college,
in those days a hefty bill, her voice
all tremolos: "The paper's calling for sleet
in Boston! Aren't you freezing?
Be careful!" October through April.

Even in her mink stole Cecelia grew cold,
colder, when Daddy's sister Marilyn
lay dying of cancer. Leaning
over her, Mother spat out,
"You brought this on yourself!"

"Now I have to drive all the way
from Long Island to Rockaway.
So much trouble because of you!"
Aunt Marilyn, thirty-three,
too sick to cry.

After Daddy died, Mother grabbed the urn,
headed south like a migratory bird,
rejoined her Montgomery girlfriends,
most of them widows by then.
She tended her roses and hibiscus.

But she couldn't escape having lived
in New York. No longer at ease
paying "the girl" eight bucks a day,

she upped the ante to thirteen, a scandal.
White-haired in the New South, was she warming?

When Mother grew tired of ashes,
she up and buried Dad, without the mourner's
Kaddish. She had loved him like fire.
Then she dumped him. Cold act,
something a poet or dictator might do.

Yet Mother was afraid of frost,
of losing her mother's lap,
her sunny toddler's lawn on Le Braun Avenue,
her native tongue of slow syllables.
There was a dry, icy spot

 inside her, and if she wasn't careful
(she rarely was), it would burn
her stylized planet, freeze her motherhood
and Brownie Scouts, forty years of Sunday School,
teaching at the Home for the Blind,

ice down the tenderness my grandma had left her—
Grandma planted next to Daddy's urn
in Montgomery's Oakhurst, not far
from poor Hank Williams, so lonesome he could die,
over in the restricted Christian section.

Grits

I didn't want to
say goodbye
to this buttery pablum
this mother's milk
in Montgomery
grits are as good
as it gets.

Mornings in our
Vincent Street kitchen
my mother brought
Alabama to Long Island
scrambled eggs and grits
fried apple slices
with powdered sugar.

She never forgave my father
for downhill mobility
for the move to New York winters
"warmed us up"
with cocoa and Fluff.

Mother also fed us
"colored people are dirty"
and "nice people never say nigger."

And when at five years old
I called old Mister Easton "nigger"
she made me go over to his apartment
and apologize.
He stood there quietly in his overalls.
The next summer he helped Mother
put up the window screens, as usual.

It's hard now to apologize
to a dead man,
but I have to start somewhere.

Mr. Easton, please forgive
my mouth.
Forgive the 1950s,
Alabama and shabby Oceanside,
our need to piss on someone.

Forgive me, Mr. Easton.
Forgive my mother.

The Ladies

When Daddy had sold enough used cars
my Southern mother bought a metal washtub,
stuck it in the basement
of our Long Island home
for the live-in maid to bathe in.
No way "the girl" could use our bath!
Just up from Alabama, the teenager sobbed
behind the door of her room.
Mommy said she cried too much,
we had to send her back.

Twelve years later,
Micky Schwerner, a Jewish college student
raised on Long Island, like me,
was murdered by the Klan in Mississippi.
I told myself *now my mother will*
understand the struggle.

"He asked for it!" she snapped.
"Should have stayed in New York
where he belonged."

Not until she was eighty, back
in Montgomery, did Mother join a protest
to restore public transportation
to the inner city.
And when a young black man—her escort
to the rally—drove up to her plush apartment,
the snowy-haired neighbors watched
with horror from behind their drapes.
Being good Southern ladies,
no one said a thing.

Horb

City etched in glass
at the Holocaust Museum.
Your name offers the roundness
of a planet,

curves of an hourglass
running out.
Your name still beautiful
though your Jews were herded off.

Horb, centuries, a moment,
no more. Out of a hundred Jews,
forty could not emigrate.
Easy to track in 1939

after the German minority census.
Sofie Sara Schwarz
Berta Sara Schwarz
The humiliation "Sara"

added to each Jewish woman's
name according to racial law.
Louis Israel Schwarz
Rubin Israel Schwarz.

My uncles stamped.
"The Nazi regime emulated
segregation laws then current
in the U.S."

In the beginning there were benches
and bathrooms: "Jews Only!"
All this frenzied purity and Horb

restricted its country air.

The forest did not disappear.
At its heart, the Jewish cemetery stands,
the stones of earlier generations overgrown:
Ernestine, Isak, Liebmann, Lina. . .

To My Poem of Hope

I don't blame you for hope,
for wanting the children
to have survived.
Because their names were not
inscribed in the "minority registration,"
you assumed they had slipped
through the net.
My dear, Horb was a hillbilly dot.
Everyone knew everyone.

Now we find this handwritten entry
by Hedwig Schwarz
in her daily book of prayer:
"On Friday, November 28, 1941
at 5:50 A.M., our dear good daughter
Hilde Sara Lemberger and our dear
good grandson Siegfried Israel Lemberger
moved away from here.
We only wish that God may watch over them
and that they stay well."

Their grandmother kept "Sara" and "Israel"
in case of Nazi eyes.
Mother and son "moved away from here"
in early darkness.
The rooster couldn't crow.

The files reveal that Hilda
and Siegfried, called "Friederle"
were deported "east for labor assignment,"
"that is to say, Riga,"
"declared dead on 4/1/1942."

Für Tot erklärt.
Pronounced by anonymous agents
with past participles on their hands.

Dear poem, if we look again,
and we must,
we will find scraps,
scrawled words, secret histories,
the cry between the lines:
"Remember. They called me Freddie.
I was six years old.
Here's what really happened."

Hedwig's Story

(details from "Rexingen Begleiter
für Friedhof und Synagoge")

Dear Great Aunt,
this fragment
reveals only that you
and your husband Louis,
along with the last elderly Jews from
Rexingen, were being transported,
that you "were unable to walk"
and "fell off the car."
Louis tried to help you but they
restrained him. August 19, 1942.

I can picture Louis more clearly than
the rest, frantic,
the train pulling away
as you lay helpless.
That hour finished him, though
he didn't die until Theresienstadt.

Some went willingly, we're told.
Nazis had promised "resettlement"
to an "old-age home."
At forty-five, you too found the way
to Theresienstadt.

You were "physically challenged."
Crippled.
Forced to stand for hours.
Did the train lurch through the back country
of Rexingen, past the lovely Neckar,
off the known world?

Outside of Prague, past slag heaps,
to Bohušovice station.
From there, prisoners had to march
three miles to Terezín.
But you couldn't walk.
Who carried you to the ghetto?

Hedwig, how did you survive?
The Martyrs Remembrance society
lists you in the camp, 1945,
Liberation.

Then the sisters of Marienhospital
in Stuttgart "cared for"
and "tended to you."
Were you a martyr,
or an ailing woman
who had finally found German mercy?

War's end left three Jews
from Rexingen.
126 had been deported.   You alone
returned to Stuttgart, "nearly blind."
You wanted to be buried
in the old Jewish cemetery,
near your mother.

This spring I placed a stone
of remembrance on your grave.

Rest, dear soul.
You survived.
Nearly blind,
you bore witness.

Survivor

The Night of Broken Glass,
thugs set fire to the Rexingen synagogue.
Scorched the Torah.
Officials blamed "outsiders."
Or kindergarteners playing with matches.
Jews on the fire brigade who doused the flames
were taken to Dachau.

Beginning of the end of three centuries
of Jewish life in Rexingen, Mühringen, Horb.
Sixty emigrated.
Ten "died on the spot."
Others were doomed to Theresienstadt,
Auschwitz, Riga.
After 1942, only one of the Schwarzes
from Horb survived deportation.

Hedwig had seen too much.
She died in Marienhospital,
Stuttgart, 1952,
fifty miles from her birthplace.
What held her to the land
of shards and ashes?

Was she lured by the
old cemetery, resting place
of her parents and grandparents?
Was the call of the dead more powerful
than *Shavei Zion*?
Perhaps the leaning firs
of the Black Forest reminded her
of her girlhood, her mother.

Nothing romantic about Terezín.
The ghetto taught her to decipher
tales of witches, children lured
to ovens. A few prisoners
had returned from Auschwitz,
told the truth about "the East."
No gingerbread houses.

But the Red Cross believed
in fairy tales.
For them, Theresienstadt
was a spa, overflowing with *Brundibár*,
soccer matches, cheerful kids.
After the official visits,
the children were transported to
Auschwitz-Birkenau.

The health care and retirement
package the Nazis had promised
turned out to be typhus, spotted fever,
starvation.

On Sunday, in hospital,
the Sisters of Saint Vincent de Paul
might have wheeled her out for a stroll.
Silence was good medicine,
they thought.

No words to ward off nightfall.
The dead were never far.

Mezuzah

In Memory, Hedwig Schwarz

In the doorpost of her house, a hollow
where the *mezuzah* used to hang.
I press my hand against the indentation,
my way of speaking to the past.

Touch the hollow where the *mezuzah*
used to hang. In Horb, Nazis renamed her street
Hitlerstrasse. My way of speaking to the past
is to listen, press the old men for answers.

1941, Jews were packed into *Hitlerstrasse*.
Now it's a winding picture postcard road,
Jew-free, pleasant as it seemed
before Nazis pressed my family into *Judenhausen*.

I press my hand against the indentation.
Over Horb, a hundred doorposts echo, hollow.

Leaning In

Three smokestacks and a sea of graves
tacked to my bulletin board: chimneys
of Terezín, and the Old Jewish Cemetery.
In Prague the dead are layered, six deep.

Unlike chimneys, the old gravestones
seem to be communing, they lean in.
Below the dead are layered, six deep.
So close, it's easier to whisper.

Communing, headstones lean in.
North of Prague, the winds carry echoes
of the Ohře, so close the dead whisper
to the river, "ashes." Remember?

North of Prague the winds bear echoes
of those transported, not in rapture.
Cattlecars. Remember, say *Kaddish*
at the Ohře. No one visits muddy ashes.

Those transported do not appear
in snapshots. There's me, my sister,
leaning toward the Ohře. Tourists
say *Kaddish*. In Prague, headstones

adorn the Old Jewish Cemetery.
Smokestacks, Terezín.

After Awhile, at Theresienstadt

(2004)

"After awhile there were so many,
that the Nazis threw the ashes of the
nameless in the Ohře."

"So the river is filled with
the dead?" a woman asks.
The eyes of her troubled daughter

grow wide. We say *Kaddish*
at the bridge overlooking the Ohře.
Only the wild-eyed daughter

knows the prayer by heart.
How long does it take a river
to forget? The rich silt

of the Ohře has much to be grateful
for, last year
its banks flooded over.

We are grateful for our young
tour guide, his fine
dreadlocks and cocoa skin,

that he speaks five languages,
one of them ours,
that his parents and grandparents,

Czech Jews, survived
the Nazis, hidden by local farmers
for four years.

Grateful that our aunt Hedwig
survived Theresienstadt,
that her bones lie in the

shady ground at Rexingen,
near her mother.
That we can find the marker

and place a stone. Thankful
for names. For breathing daughters.
Blessed are You, O God.

Notes

"Monsieur Moreau"

The Paris police rounded up 12,884 Jews on July 16-17, 1942. Those without families were sent to Drancy. The remaining 9,000, including 4,000 children, were penned up in the sports stadium Vélodrome d'Hiver before being transported to Auschwitz. (Lucy S. Dawidowicz, *The War Against the Jews*, New York: Holt, Rinehart, and Winston, 1975, p. 362).

"To My Poem of Hope"

In 1939, German Jews were required to fill out minority registration forms. These can be viewed at the United States Holocaust Memorial Museum in Washington, D.C.

The prayerbook is housed in the Rexingen Jewish archives. Dr. Gilya Schmidt translated the inscription.

In 1941, the Nazis murdered 26,500 Latvian Jews in the Riga ghetto to make room for transports of more than 20,000 Jews from the Reich and elsewhere (1941-1942). Only a few hundred survived.

"Hedwig's Story"

"Rexingen Begleiter für Friedhof und Synagoge," ("Rexingen Companion to the Cemetery and the Synagogue") is available from the Rexingen Jewish archives. Dr. Gilya Schmidt translated the section on Hedwig Schwarz. The Terezín Martyr's Remembrance Society offered information about Hedwig Schwarz, as did the sisters of Marienhospital in Stuttgart.

In late 1941, the Nazis turned the town of Theresienstadt, or Terezín, sixty kilometers northwest of Prague, into a ghetto/transit camp. Theresienstadt became a conduit to Auschwitz and other extermination camps. Elderly Jews from the Reich, as well as children, and distinguished artists, were among those sent to the ghetto. 155,000 people passed through the camp; 118,00 perished, of which 35,000 died in Theresienstadt from disease, malnutrition, and torture. (Vojtěk Blodig, *Terezín: Terezín in the Final Solution of the Jewish Question: 1941-1945*, 2003).

"Survivor"

Many details in this poem were provided by Bernhard Sayer, the Jewish archivist for Rexingen/Horb, in a personal interview, March 22, 2004.

"The Night of Broken Glass," *Kristallnacht*, was a state-sanctioned pogrom that took place across Germany on November 8 and 9, 1938.

(Some data in the second stanza is from *Pinkas Hakehillot: Encylopaedia of Jewish Communities from their foundation till after the Holocaust*, "Germany." Yad Vashem, Jerusalem, 1986, pp. 76-78.)

"Mezuzah"

Mezuzah, a small prayer scroll housed in protective casing, is nailed to the right doorpost as a sign of a Jewish home, to invite God's blessing. The prayers include the *Sh'ema* ("Hear O Israel") and passages from *Deuteronomy* 6:4-9 and 11:13-21.

"After Awhile"

The dead were buried in individual graves until August 1942, then in mass graves. In October, 1942, the crematorium was put into operation. Ashes were stored and marked. In November, 1944, all the ashes were thrown into the Ohře as well as into a mud pit bordering the camp. (See Blodig, *Terezín*, p. 63, as well as *Art, Music, and Education as Strategies for Survival: Theresienstadt, 1941-45*, ed. Anne D. Dutlinger, New York: Herodias, 2001, p. 179.)

Marilyn Kallet is the author of ten other books. Her poems have appeared in hundreds of publications, including *New Letters, Prairie Schooner,* and *Tar River Poetry.* Kallet has won the Tennessee Arts Commission Literary Fellowship in poetry and was named Outstanding Woman in the Arts by the Knoxville YWCA. She is the poetry editor for *New Millennium Writings* and holds the Hodges Chair for Distinguished Teaching at the University of Tennessee in Knoxville, where she directed the creative writing program for seventeen years.